Contents

Words in **bold** are explained in the glossary!

Telling the time

At last, it is Saturday! We have been planning a trip to the zoo all week.

At the zoo there will be different things to see at different times. Let's check what we know about telling the time. We don't want to miss anything!

Hours and minutes

The little hand on a clock tells us what **hour** it is. This one is pointing at the 3. The big hand tells us about the **minutes**. Because it is pointing at the 12, the time is exactly 3 **o'clock**. Remember that the big hand on 12 means o'clock.

What time is it?

Now the little hand has passed the 3. The big hand is pointing at the 6. So the time is **half-past** 3. Don't forget there are 60 minutes in one hour!

Can you tell the time on these clocks?

Instead of half-past 3, we sometimes say three-thirty.

It is quarter-past

Let's see what happens when the big hand points at the 3. What time does it become then?

Quarter-past 10

The little hand on this clock is pointing just past the 10.

The big hand is now pointing at the 3. This means the time is **quarter-past** 10.

It is called 'quarter-past' because the big hand has moved quarter way around the clock face.

Quarter-past 1

The little hand is just past the 1. The big hand tells us it is quarter-past.

Digital clocks

This digital clock does not have any hands.

The first number tells you the hour is 8 o'clock.

The second number tells you it is 15 **minutes** past 8 o'clock. 15 minutes is a **quarter of an hour**. This means it is quarter-past 8.

Quarter-past 8 is also called eight-fifteen.

Let's see what happens when the big hand points at the 9. Can you see how the little hand has moved?

Quarter-to 5

On this watch the little hand is almost pointing at the 5.

The big hand is now pointing at the 9. It has a quarter of the clock face to get to number 12, which means o'clock. When the big hand has moved all the way to 12, the time will be 5 o'clock, but right now the time is **quarter-to** 5.

Quarter-to 9

The little hand on this clock is almost at the 9. The big hand tells us it is quarter-to.

Digital clocks

This digital clock says 8:45. This tells us that it is 45 minutes past 8 o'clock. It also tells us that it is 15 minutes to the next hour. This means it is quarter-to 9.

My day at the zoo

The alarm clock is ringing, it's time to get up.
I am very excited about
going to the zoo today.

Time for breakfast

Half-past 7
First, we have pancakes
for breakfast. Then it is
time to clean our teeth
and get dressed.

Time to get ready

Quarter-past 8

Dad is making some sandwiches for our lunch. He says we need to leave in 45 minutes.

Time to go

9 o'clock

It is time for us to go now. Mum says we had better walk quickly. The bus leaves in 15 minutes.

Times before 12 o'clock noon are called 'am'.

Morning at the zoo

It took us half an hour to get to the zoo.
Now it is quarter-to 10. Let's visit the apes
and monkeys first!

Monkey time

10 o'clock

After a quarter of an
hour, we find the
monkeys. Look, there's
a baby monkey
on its mum's back!

One of the other
monkeys is still
having breakfast!

Elephant bath time

Quarter-to 11

We hurry to see the elephants next. Their bath time is half-past 10. We are 15 minutes late but we still get to see the last elephant having its bath.

High and mighty

Half-past 11

At half-past 11, the giraffes are already eating. It must be almost lunchtime.

What time do you eat your lunch?

Feeding time at the zoo

We are hungry after seeing the giraffes eat lunch.
We eat our sandwiches while we watch the penguins.

Fish for lunch!

12 o'clock
It is **noon** and the penguins
are hungry, too. Look! One
of them is eating a fish.

Bamboo for lunch

Quarter-past 1

The panda is still eating lunch at 1:15. Bamboo is her main food. We watch the panda for 30 minutes.

Tiger time

Quarter-to 2

Now we visit the tiger. Can you see him? His stripes make him hard to spot in the long grass.

Times after 12 o'clock noon are called 'pm'.

Afternoon at the zoo

My day at the zoo is going by quickly. I'm getting a little tired, but there are many more animals to visit before it is time to go home.

Half-past 2

We decide to have a rest and watch the sharks. They are in a big tank of water called an aquarium. Look how huge they are! We watch the sharks for **half an hour**.

Afternoon rest

3 o'clock
Look! The lioness and her cubs are resting too.

Rhino watching

Quarter-to 4
Quick! We just have time to see the rhino. The bus home leaves in 15 minutes.

Remember that 15 minutes is a quarter of an hour.

Evening and night

On the way home we talk about all the animals we saw. My favourite was the lion! Mum liked the giraffe. Dad liked the sharks.

Back at home

Quarter-to 5

When we get home, Mum starts getting dinner ready. It will be dinner time in 45 minutes.

Dinner time

Half-past 5

As we eat, Mum tells us that the zoo takes care of many animals who cannot survive in the wild.

Bed time

Quarter-past 7

I am tucked into bed with my cuddly new lion. It is still a quarter of an hour before my usual bedtime, but I am very, very tired. I had a fun day at the zoo.

What time do you go to bed?

Time facts

There are lots of things to learn about hours and minutes. Take a look at some of them here.

> ## Hours
> Remember each day has 24 hours.

Times between midnight and noon end in **am**. So 3:30am is when you are asleep!

Times between noon and midnight end in **pm**. So 3:30pm is in the afternoon.

Minutes

Each hour has 60 minutes.

After 15 minutes it is quarter-past the hour.

After 45 minutes it is quarter-to the next hour.

After 30 minutes it is half-past the hour.

Each minute has 60 seconds!

Time to remember

What can you remember about the time?
Have a go at these fun puzzles.

Meal times
Match the meals with their time.

Lunch

Breakfast

Dinner

7:30am

1:00pm

5:30pm

22

Time it game!

How long do you think it takes to do each of these things?
Ask an adult to time you using a clock or watch.

Cleaning your teeth.

Getting dressed.

Eating your breakfast.

Tidying your bedroom.

Do you have your own clock or watch?

Glossary

Do you remember what the times on these clocks are?

am This is used to show that a time is between midnight and noon, so 9am is 9 o'clock in the morning.

Half an hour An hour has 60 minutes, so half of an hour is 30 minutes.

Half-past This is used when telling the time. It tells you that the big minute hand is pointing exactly at the six, and half of the hour has passed.

Hour An hour is 60 minutes. There are 24 hours in every day.

Minute A minute is 60 seconds. There are 60 minutes in every hour.

Noon Noon is the middle of the day. It is 12 o'clock. Sometimes it is called midday.

O'clock This is used when telling the time. It tells you that the big minute hand is pointing exactly at the 12. The time is exactly the number the little hand is pointing at, such as 8 o'clock.

pm This is used to show that a time is between noon and midnight, so 9pm is 9 o'clock at night.

Quarter of an hour An hour has 60 minutes, so a quarter of an hour is 15 minutes.

Quarter-past This is used when telling the time. It tells you that the big minute hand is pointing exactly at the three, and a quarter of the hour has passed.

Quarter-to This is used when telling the time. It tells you that the big minute hand is pointing exactly at the nine and that it is only a quarter of an hour until the next hour begins.

Week A week is seven days. They are Monday, Tuesday, Wednesday, Thursday, Friday, Saturday and Sunday.